THE WISE ONE

SPIRITUAL WISDOM
FOR EVERYDAY LIVING

Rosamonde

ZORBA BOOKS

Published in India by Zorba Books, 2017

Website: www.zorbabooks.com
Email: info@zorbabooks.com

Copyright © Rosamonde

ISBN Print Book : 978-93-86407-87-0
ISBN eBook : 978-93-86407-88-7

All rights reserved. No part of this book may be reproduced or transmitted in any form or by any means, electronic or mechanical, including photocopying, recording, or by an information storage and retrieval system—except by a reviewer who may quote brief passages in a review to be printed in a magazine, newspaper, or on the Web—without permission in writing from the copyright owner.

Although the author and publisher have made every effort to ensure the accuracy and completeness of information contained in this book, we assume no responsibility for errors, inaccuracies, omissions, or any inconsistencies herein. Any slights on people, places, or organizations are unintentional.

Zorba Books Pvt. Ltd.(opc)
Gurgaon, INDIA

Printed at Repro Knowledgecast Limited, Thane

Dedicated to

ALL MY SPIRITUAL TEACHERS
SEEN AND UNSEEN

Author

Rosamonde is a metaphysical, spiritual explorer. Her exploration started when she was ten and started to ask the questions "Who am I and where do I come from?" This quest has taken her to all corners of the world. Working and living in many cultures and environments, like the Cairo slums, working in bars in Lebanon and living on the kibbutz in Israel. To ashrams in India, where she studied to be a yoga teacher.

Rosamonde has studied buddhism, bhakti yoga, siddha yoga, reiki, hypnotherapy, christianity, mindfulness, and the law of attraction.

Life experiences and adventures have contributed immensely to her education. She meditates daily, and constantly practices listening to her intuition.

To get in touch with the author please email to her on serendpty46@gmail.com

www.authorrosamonde.com

INTRODUCTION

Several years ago, I read the book 'The Prophet' by Khalil Gibran.

Then I thought I would like to write a more modern version similar to that book.

Where a Wise One, wisely answers questions asked by people in a community.

Some ten years ago after meditating, the words for the chapter on LOVE came to me.

Thus starting the beginning of this book.

From there began a slow journey of doubting myself, writing, rewriting, discarding. Saying to myself that my words were not as valid as others.

For many years I put the book to sleep.

Until the day I realised that every book was written through each authors experiences and insights

And that my insights and experiences were just as valid.

I felt that if there was one chapter that resonated with people, it was worth publishing.

So here I am dear reader, introducing you to my simple, small book on Spiritual Wisdom for every day living.

The Wise One

Contents

1. Acceptance — 11
2. Birthing — 13
3. Children — 15
4. Compassion — 17
5. Death — 19
6. Dreams — 21
7. Family — 23
8. Forgiveness — 25
9. Freedom — 27
10. Friends — 29
11. God — 31
12. Heaven — 33
13. Joy — 35
14. Judgement — 37
15. Kindness — 39
16. Laughter — 41

17. Learning	43
18. Lies	45
19. Love	47
20. Magic	49
21. Money	51
22. Nature	53
23. Realities	55
24. Relationships	57
25. Self Value	59
26. Stillness	61
27. Thoughts	63
28. Time	65
29. Words	67
30. Work	69

THE WISE ONE

Wise One
Acceptance

The Greatest Gift You Can Give To Another
And Yourself, Is Acceptance

Acceptance

An old man asked, " Wise One speak to us of acceptance."

The Wise one said,"The greatest gift you can give to another and to yourself is acceptance.

For as you accept yourself, as you are right now, so too will you accept others for who they are.

Acceptance filled with love is truly the most wondrous communion with another.

From there many rewarding deep friendships have been created.

I say to you, acceptance is the knowledge, that we are all on a personal journey of understanding and exploring of ourselves, while here on earth and who are we to judge another's journey."

Wise One Birthing

It Is So Important For The Soul Of The Baby To Be Housed In A Safe, Loving, Supportive, Environment During Pregnancy.

The Wise One

Birthing

A mother asked, "Wise One please tell us about birthing."

The Wise One said, "It is so important for the soul of the baby to be housed in a safe, loving, supportive environment, during pregnancy.

Thus it is necessary for the mother to be given the physical, loving support that she needs.

Yet many mothers do not receive this, thus creating a fractured energy in the soul, of the baby.

There are times the mother does not wish for the child and the soul energy of the baby, knows exactly how the parents feel about their entrance.

I say to you, think carefully before becoming a parent, for it is the most responsible role you will ever have.

If it is your time to be a parent, spiritually and physically prepare yourself, so that you are in a supportive environment and can be at peace with this journey."

Wise One
Children

Your Children Are The Eyes Of Your Tomorrow.
They Have Innocent Visions
Of Worlds You Have Long Forgotten.

The Wise One

Children

And a parent said, "Wise One speak to us of children."

The Wise One said, "Your children are the eyes of your tomorrow.

They have innocent visions of worlds you have long forgotten.

They are the arrows that shoot from your bow into the tomorrows to create new dreams.

They come to you, to remind you of your long forgotten innocence.

Their hearts are pure and their eyes see the truth that you have forgotten.

I say to you, as you introduce them to the world and its many ways, remind them not to judge themselves by worldly values.

But to remember their truth and their spiritual beauty.

If you do this you have truly fulfilled your duty as parents."

Wise One
Compassion

Compassion Is The Expression Of The Soul In Action And Understanding

The Wise One

Compassion

A social worker asked, "Wise One speak to us of compassion."

The Wise One said, "Compassion is the expression of the soul in action and understanding.

It is when your heart reaches out to another that compassion rises in your soul.

For compassion is the expression of one to another, saying, I care.

Knowing that we are all one and what is happening to you could easily happen to me.

In today's world, it is so easy to turn the other way and not get involved.

Few of you even ask are you alright, can I help? So many like to tell the other what to do, rather than listen and try to understand where that person is in their being and from that understanding offer assistance.

I say to you, next time you meet another in need, quietly give of yourself in a way that does not undermine their dignity, nor do it for recognition, or self validation. Just take time and listen."

Wise One
Death

When You Realize Your Journey
Here On Earth Is Only Temporary.
Instead Of Fearing The End,
See It As A New Beginning

The Wise One

Death

A funeral director asked "Wise One speak to us of death."

The Wise One said,"As you are born so you daily go towards your death.

This you innately know and yet many of you so fear the inevitable.

Your body, is like a cloak, that covers your soul, as it journeys through this earthly life and when it has finished its journey here, it will transcend to another realm, cloaked in another vibration.

When you realize your journey here on earth is only temporary.

Instead of fearing the end, see it as the end of one adventure, only to be replaced by another.

I say to you, when your time has come, embrace the light and let the love that surrounds you take you to your new journey."

Wise One
Dreams

It Is Through Your Dreams That You Create
Your Tomorrow.
For Without Dreams Hopes And Wishes What
Would Life Be

Dreams

A young boy asked, "Wise One speak to me of dreams and ambition."

The Wise One said, "It is through your dreams that you create your tomorrow. For without dreams, hopes and wishes what would life be.

Creating your dreams into physical reality is an intertwined web of imagining, knowledge, combined with action.

For dreams without action remain only dreams hidden within your disappointed heart.

I say to you, be mentally and emotionally prepared to receive and become your dreams, for they can easily disappear from your reality."

Wise One
Family

Your Family Is The Interwoven Web That
Surrounds You At Birth
It Is Through The family you form
Your perspective On Life

The Wise One

Family

A grand parent asked, "Wise One speak to us of families."

The Wise One said, "Your family is the interwoven web that surrounds you at birth. It is through the family you form your perspective on life.

For some the web is filled with love, nurturing and support. While for others it can be fraught with conflict, abuse and confusion.

It is the journey the soul takes to have many varied experiences on earth.

For each of you this experience is unique to you and the mother who gives birth to you.

Many may say they hate their family and wonder why they chose to incarnate with this family.

Only on a soul memory will you know why.

I say to you, for every one of you who plan to have a family or have created one.

Honour the responsibility and challenges it will bring and throughout the journey let love be the most important ingredient behind every decision you make."

Wise One
Forgiveness

It is In the Forgiving Of Another
And Of Yourself,
That Releases You From
Your Anger, Hate And, Blame
That Binds You To The Past

The Wise One

Forgiveness

A divorced woman asked, "Wise One speak to us of forgiveness."

The Wise One said, "Forgiveness is an act of compassion towards another.

It is in the forgiving of another and of yourself, that releases you from your anger, hate and blame that binds you to the past.

For what benefit is it to you, to hold on to these past wrongs doings that keep your life on hold.

If you keep reflecting on the hurt another has done to you, so too will you draw it again into your now.

I say to you, through forgiveness you will find freedom to live your life anew."

Wise One
Freedom

The Greatest Freedom Is
The Freedom Within Yourself

The Wise One

Freedom

And a nomad asked, "Wise One speak to us of freedom."

The Wise One said, "The greatest freedom is the freedom within yourself.

When your mind, body and spirit are aligned in total harmony, there is no greater freedom.

As most people are not there, they look for freedom from external situations.

There are endless freedom desires that fill your heart and minds.

Yet so few of you are free from your constant recurring thoughts.

Everyone of you is free. Free to choose your thoughts and feelings in the moment.

Free to change your limiting beliefs and with this knowledge you can create a life of unlimited possibilities of freedom and fulfil dreams long held secret.

I say to you, as you wake in the morning, embrace the stillness of your mind and in that stillness you will sense your souls freedom, which will carry you through your day."

Wise One
Friends

Friends Are The Jewels In
Your Lives For Without Them Your
Life Would Be Very Empty.

The Wise One

Friends

A teenage girl asked, "Wise One speak to us of friends."

The Wise One said, "Friends are the jewels in your life.

For without them your life would be very empty.

It is through this interchange your life is enriched with variety, fun, sharing, caring, love and adventures.

They are the sizzle and richness that nurtures your life.

True friends will support you through life's journey and are there to listen to you.

They are also there to tell you truths that you may not want to hear.

I say to you, The most important thing is for you to become a good friend to others and then you will attract this to yourself."

Wise One
God

God Is TheEnergy That
Reverberates
ThroughoutThe Universes.

The Wise One

God

A Priest asked "Wise One speak to us of God."

The Wise One said, "God is the energy that reverberates throughout the universes.

There is nothing that is in the universes that is not God.

Your religions have taught you that a part of you is of God and another part that is not.

I say to you all of you is of God. There is not one thought, or act or cell in your body that is not of God."

"But what about all of the evil thoughts and acts that we do," the priest asked.

"My dear friend, it is because you do not live in your godliness that you do these 'ungodly acts'

For if you truly lived in your godliness the desire to do these harmful acts would not rise inside you.

I say to you, come back to the God within and from there live your life."

Wise One
Heaven

The Vibration, You Call Heaven Is
Filled WithA Sweet Love
That Totally Embraces
And Supports You On Your Eternal Journey.

Heaven

And a monk asked, "Wise One speak to us of heaven."

The Wise One said, "Heaven is not a place, rather it is an energy that surrounds you on your soul's journey home.

It is a vibration, filled with a sweet love that totally embraces and supports you on your eternal journey.

For many of you there is a constant yearning to go home to this energy, for this is where your soul comes from.

Some of you ask, can heaven be experienced here on earth. I say yes, but not in all its magical essence that lies beyond the physical.

I say to you, the most important thing for you to do, is to return to your soul essence and there you will have a taste of heaven."

Wise One
Joy

Joy Is Your Spirit Expressing
Itself In Spontaneous Happiness.

The Wise One

Joy

A counsellor asked, "Wise One speak to us of joy."

The Wise One said, "Joy is the inner essence of your being.

It is the enthusiasm that surges through your body. Filling your imagination with limitless thoughts and ideas.

While you watch children play and see their spontaneus creative ways they interact with each other, laughing at what seems silly things. They show you natural joy at play.

Joy is like sparkling water that rises inside you, expressing itself in laughter, fun and light heartedness.

This is your natural state and because you have lost touch with it, you seek it outside yourself through your relationships and external play.

It is through your meditation you can touch this inner joy, that turns to bliss.

I say to you, take time to come home to your inner joy and see how wonderful your life will unfold."

Wise One
Judgement

Judgement Is The Limitation Of The Ego Mind
Placing False Perceptions On Another.

The Wise One

Judgement

A judge asked, "Wise One speak to us of judgement."

The Wise One said,"As you judge others so too will they judge you.

Judgement is the limitation of the ego mind placing false perceptions on another.

For when another does not perform or act according to our own expectations, we place limited observations on them.

There is not one of you that truly knows, the making and complexity of another, or what truly resides in their soul.

You witness their expressions through their actions and their words and from that you judge each other.

Only a few have the insight that really knows what is going on inside another.

I say to you, before you quickly come to judge another take time to know them."

Wise One
Kindness

Kindness Is Thoughtfulness
Expressed Through Action.

The Wise One

Kindness

An elderly lady asked, " Wise One speak to us of kindness."

The Wise One said, "Kindness is thoughtfulness expressed through action.

If it were not for these kindly acts the world would not exist.

Kindness is when you open your heart to another and offer a helping hand.

Not for recognition but because you desire to do this.

Throughout the world there are many random acts of kindness, that touch many hearts leaving memories of gratitude.

I say to you, open your hearts and share in random acts of kindness. It will fill your heart with much joy."

Wise One
Laughter

Laughter Is The Nectar Of Life
It Is The Sweetness That
Flavours Your World.

The Wise One

Laughter

A comedian asked, "Wise One speak to us of laughter."

The Wise One said, "Laughter is the nectar of life.

It is the sweetness that flavours your world.

For without laughter, life is devoid of any joy and exuberance.

It is the light hearted moments of laughter with another that lifts your spirits and fills the moment with joy.

The greatest gift you can give to others and yourself is to find humour, even in moments of darkness.

Laughter is the secret elixir to every coming together with others.

I say to you, fill your day with laughter and feel the rays of happiness shimmer through your day."

Wise One
Learning

From The Day You Are Born And Before,
You Are Constantly Learning Through
Your Experiences And Observations.

The Wise One

Learning

And a school teacher asked, "Wise One speak to us of learning."

The Wise One said, "From the day you are born and before, you are constantly learning, through your experiences and observations. For this is the way the soul choses to experience life on earth. It is through your feeling body that most knowledge is gained.

As you progress through life and formal education is introduced to you. Your soul learns to absorb this knowledge, often enjoying the play.

As you are moulded by this information your mind and thinking abilities develop. Often losing touch with the creative soul that lies within.

You are encouraged to regurgitate information, rather than to create it.

It is in the schools that entertain the idea of the creative soul of the child and creates knowledge in a natural, creative way, that the child will shine and enjoy their time in school.

For learning needs to be enjoyed and not made a chore.

I say to you, create your schools to be exciting learning places that your children look forward to attend."

Wise One
Lies

As You Tell A Lie To Another So Too You Lie To Yourself And It Is These Lies You Tell Yourself That Give Lasting Scars On Your Souls Memory.

The Wise One

Lies

A teenager asked, "Wise One speak to us of lies"

The Wise One said "It is the lies you tell yourself that scars your being more than anything else.

For most of you tell lies as a way to survive in your world. Lies are so part of everything in your culture you take them as normal.

Your society has been built on illusions and lies. Thus the truth has become something of a myth.

As you tell a lie to another, so too you lie to yourself and it is these lies you tell yourself that give lasting scars on your souls memory.

Yet your heart cries out for your own truth, the truth that lies within you.

As you go through life and get caught up in the illusions of life, your truth gets buried causing much discontent, as your soul knows this is not where your essence is.

I say to you, have courage and practise speaking your truth throughout your life."

Wise One
Love

Love Is The Tremulous Energy That Lies
Behind The Creation Of Your Lives.

The Wise One

Love

A young woman asked, "Wise One speak to us of love."

The Wise One said, "Love is the tremulous energy that is behind the creation of your lives.

It is your true essence and that is why you chase it.

For without it, there is no reason for you to live.

It is the force that creates the rising sun and setting day.

It is the joy and wonder of everything that is in you and without you.

It is the birth of everything new and the passing of every done thing. It is you, it is you. You are love.

But because you know not this, you look to others for love and this often causes you so much pain, hurt, expectations and illusions that are not true love.

I say to you, true love knows no limits or expectations.

True love does not judge or condemn.

True love does not give, then takeaway.

True love never disappears

True Love Just is

Wise One
Magic

Magic Is Wonder That Fills Your Heart
And Eyes.
It Is The Lens Through Which
You Perceive Life.

The Wise One

Magic

A magician asked, "Wise One speak to us of magic."

The Wise One said, "Magic is the wonder that fills your heart and eyes. It is the lens through which you perceive life.

Each one of you was born with magic in your heart.

Yet over time it slowly disappears, as you close your eyes to its wonder.

Magic is the gift our children give us as we watch them in spontaneous play.

Like a magician, who can make things disappear then with the wave of his hand makes it appear again.

So too are the fleeting moments of magic, that appear and quickly disappear in your mind.

Leaving some of you disillusioned with life, as you grow to believe only in what you can see with your physical eyes.

I say to you, only when you allow yourselves to become more childlike, will you see the magic in your lives."

Wise One
Money

Money Is An Energy Exchange For Goods And Services

The Wise One

Money

A banker asked, "Wise One speak to us of money".

The Wise One said, "Money is an energy exchange for services and goods.

It is a commodity that often controls and governs your lives while on earth. For many souls it is an imprisonment, that kills their hidden desire for freedom.

Money has become the golden idol that has many lay awake at night wondering how to make it or hold on to it. For many, no matter how much they have it is not enough.

Because they feel a lack inside themselves, they look to money to fill the void.

There truly is enough money for everyone. But, because the way it is distributed and controlled, it rarely gets shared to all.

I say to you, value money for how it provides for you and your family.

Do not let it imprison your lives by having you always wanting for more.

Nor envy those who have more than you, or look down on those who have less."

Wise One
Nature

Nature Is TheGreatest Gift The
Great Creator Has Given
The Human Race To Embrace.

Nature

A gardener asked, "Wise One speak to us of nature."

The Wise One said, "Nature is the greatest gift the great creator has given humanity, to embrace.

To feed, shelter and clothe them. Nature feeds your planet with air, nutrients, and unseen energies that heals the human body and soul. Yet because it has been the quiet giver to all, what has humanity done with the great creator's gift. They have tried to mould it to suit themselves. In their ignorance they chop down forests to make way for farms, when they could have had both.

They dam the rivers, poison the ground with chemicals, and extract oil and minerals that holds her together.

Then humanity wonders why mother earth explodes around them. The time has come that mother earth will spill and spit everyone out, for she can no longer suffer the pain that humans have inflicted upon her.

There is a rising consciousness of some who know this and seek ways to turn the tide. She asks those who care, to take time to teach and share nature with their children, so they can become better caretakers of the earth.

I say to you, for every flower and tree you plant with love, she is grateful. For she feels the energy from your heart through your hands and thanks you."

Wise One
Realities

There are Realities Beyond The Realities
That You Now Perceive
That Are Far Greater Than You Will Ever
Know In Your Human Form.

The Wise One

Realities

A quantum physicist asked, "Wise One tell us about other realities."

The Wise One said, "There are realities beyond the realities that you now perceive, that are far greater than you will ever know in your human form.

The infinite sky that you see with your naked eye, is just a speck of what the creator has in store for you in other dimensions.

Your physical reality is such a small aspect of the greater picture.

It is only in your dreams you allow your consciousness to flow freely to see other realities.

As the universes are far greater than you can perceive so too are you.

I say to you, it is only by going within can you experience your infiniteness."

Wise One
Relationships

It Is Through Your Everyday Relating
With Each Other
That Brings Richness To
You're Lives.

The Wise One

Relationships

A young woman asked, "Wise One speak to us of relationships."

The Wise One said, "It is through your everyday relating with each other that brings richness to your lives.

It is this interchange and exchange that is the major priority of your lives, as this is what gives your life purpose.

If you choose to isolate yourself from people, you fail to develop the most important aspects of yourselves, the ability to relate and love another.

When love blossoms between two people and the relationship becomes one of two souls soaring on the same cloud, relating then becomes a unity blessed in the essence of love.

For there is no greater time when you love someone, so much, that you only see their beauty.

As you bask in each other's love, remember to respect each other's differences and try not to mould one another into expected forms.But rather encourage each other to blossom and develop in your own unique ways.

Each one of you desires to give and receive love, as this is your natural state.

So I say to you, fill your life with loving, caring, relationships, for it those relationships that will eventually heal the world."

Wise One
Self Value

It Is When Mind, Body And Soul
Are In Harmony,
That One Experiences One's True Value.

The Wise One

Self Value

A young man asked,"Wise One speak to us of self value."

The Wise One said,"Many of you say you love yourselves, you value yourselves. But truly you don't.

Even those who give the air of self confidence, often do not truly value themselves.

Because of that, most of you look for external validation, from others.

The true sense of self value comes from within.

It comes from knowing and living in your inner source. It is a state of being.

Self value is when mind, body and spirit are in harmony,

For those of you who are not in that state, saying and singing words of self love, will only temporarily help.

I say to you, it is better to take time to be still, calm the mind and feel the richness of your inner self and there you will find your true self value."

Wise One
Stillness

It Is Within The Stillness Of
Your Life That You Will Find Your
Greatest Peace.

The Wise One

Stillness

A meditator asked, "Wise One speak to us of stillness."

The Wise One said, "It is within the stillness of your life that you will find your greatest peace.

For how easy it is to rush here and there busying yourself, never stopping to just be.

It is in the stillness of yourself, your greatest imagination arises and you feel the greatest depth of your soul.

As you sit in that stillness, a peace overtakes the chatting mind, filling you with a deep contentment.

Our journey through life, is to learn, to just be

I say to you, take twenty minutes out of your day to meditate, and just be, to touch the peace that lies within."

Wise One
Thoughts

Your Thoughts Are The Silent Words
You Say To Yourself.
They Are The Constant Dialogue
That Goes Through Your Mind.

The Wise One

Thoughts

A psychologist said, "Wise One speak to us of thoughts."

The Wise One said, "Your thoughts are the silent words you say to yourself.

They are the constant dialogue that goes through your mind.

Thoughts are the mirrors through which you perceive the world and yourself.

Some like to say you are only thought manifested.

But I say, you are spirit vibrating through thought.

Your task is to become the master of your thoughts, rather than the prisoner. For only you can change them.

Your soul takes on cultural and family beliefs systems through which to experience life.

As you progress through life, your beliefs and thoughts may change. Creating a different reality for you.

I say to you, take time to meditate to listen to the quiet murmur of your soul. For that is where you will find your truth, hidden beyond your chattering mind."

Wise One
Time

It Is When You Live InUniversal Time That
Resides In Your Soul
That You Will Become Aware Of
Whom You Truly Are.

The Wise One

Time

A clock maker said,"Wise One speak to us of time."

The Wise One said,"Time is an illusion created by humans, to try and understand nature and control their day.

You are so conditioned by the clock, that you have forgotten to listen to your internal time.

Life has you running from one appointment to another, creating a stressful life.

The more you live in the present, focusing on the now. The more you will live in the universal flow.

It is when you live with universal time that resides in your soul that you will become aware of whom you truly are.

I say to you, be in the now, live in the now, play in the now."

Wise One Words

Words Are The Vibrational Sounds
You Use To Express Yourselves.

The Wise One

Words

An author asked, Wise One speak to us of words"

The Wise One said, "Words are the vibrational sounds you use to express what lies in your heart.

Like all vibrations they have ripple effects, that can either lift or destroy another's spirit.

Speak not words of gossip or criticism of another.

Rather speak words of positive impressions of each other.

For as you speak of others, so too will they speak of you.

So I say to you, when you speak to another speak words of encouragement and kindness.

Speak to them in a way you would like to be spoken to."

Wise One
Work

It Is In Your Everyday Tasks
That You Find Purpose To Your Day.

The Wise One

Work

And a labourer asked,"Wise One speak to us of work."

The Wise One said,"It is in your everyday tasks that you find purpose to your day.

For what is a life wasted in idleness, with nothing to do. Rarely contributing to life in any way.

Work gives you opportunity to learn and develop new skills, to expand your knowledge into new areas.

For many work is necessary to provide for yourselves and your family. Thus often creating a rod to your lives.

For others, work is creative and fulfilling, giving meaning to their lives.

It is the attitude to which you approach your work. Be it sweeping a floor or running a corporation.

In the eyes of God all work is equal.

For in the running of your world, the garbage collector's job is just as important as the leader of your countries.

I say to you, be cheerful at your work, no matter what you do, as that will bring joy to your day."

www.ingramcontent.com/pod-product-compliance
Lightning Source LLC
Chambersburg PA
CBHW071410160426
42813CB00085B/733